Margaret E. Blackburn

Things a Pastor's Wife Can Do

Margaret E. Blackburn

Things a Pastor's Wife Can Do

ISBN/EAN: 9783337715694

Printed in Europe, USA, Canada, Australia, Japan

Cover: Foto ©Lupo / pixelio.de

More available books at **www.hansebooks.com**

Things a Pastor's Wife Can Do

BY

ONE OF THEM

PHILADELPHIA

American Baptist Publication Society

MDCCCXCVIII

From the Society's own Press

CONTENTS

THINGS A PASTOR'S WIFE CAN DO

I

CHOSEN AS A WIFE

A LETTER came to me recently from a friend who has been asked by a young pastor to enter our ranks. She says she feels utterly unfit for the great responsibilities so soon to be hers, and that she will often be obliged to ask advice from those of us who are older and more experienced. Her letter reminded me of an article I thought of writing when I was a young pastor's wife, but my pen exhausted itself on the title ''Pastors' Wives and Sweethearts,'' and it has taken all these years for the accumulation of courage sufficient to attack this important subject.

The writer of this letter had no thought

of being a pastor's wife until she met
this young minister and their love became
mutual. To my mind she could have no
better fitness. A pastor's wife who car-
ries about her an official air is, to say the
least, a very disagreeable person, and a
minister who marries a woman simply because he thinks, or is told, that she will
make a good wife for a pastor, makes the
mistake of his life. Any healthy, hope-
ful, happy, devoted Christian girl is capa-
ble of making the ideal pastor's wife. A
pastor should not choose his wife as he
does his pulpit suit, or silk hat, or even as
he does his concordance. Any girl who
has health and education, and loves Christ
more than she does the world, can soon
train into service and need have no fear of
failure.

Ministers wives who are failures are few,
and they would have been failures if their
husbands had been in other professions or
in business. The same rules for the choice
of a wife apply in the ministry that are
absolutely necessary for happiness in any
other calling in life.

Two people who are to be intimate

friends for life should have similar tastes. It is not necessary to agree in everything. In fact, there is more "spice" in slight differences where questions are simply matters of opinion, and right and wrong are not involved.

We once knew a notable housewife and exquisite needle woman, but if there had not been a newspaper in the world she would not have cared. Her husband, on the other hand, thought there was no greater luxury than a book, and he was so ignorant of practical affairs that in carving for guests he left the choice meat on the platter. Who could expect this banker and his wife to be happy? She longed for a lover, and he came home simply for his meals and a quiet place in which to read. She would have worked or denied herself anything for a material blessing or to give to the church, but the money "wasted in books" wrecked their lives.

No one can tell what disease the future may hold in store for either the husband or wife, but a healthy person should not marry one with frail health. More happiness will come from the union of two invalids, for then they can condole and truly sympathize with each other. If one is rich and the other poor, for real happiness the wife had better be the poorer. Equality in earthly possessions is to be desired for the most perfect happiness.

While a pastor does not look for the label on a girl, he should not utterly disregard common sense in the choice of a wife, and look for happiness and success in a flirt, or for a girl whose heart is in the world, or for one who is utterly selfish. Worldly men prefer Christian wives. In choosing, the pastor should pray for this wisdom.

If the writer has had any share in the success of her pastor it is not because she felt called to the place. In fact, a little scene in her girlhood is recalled with amusement. A young man called one afternoon and brought with him an offer of marriage. He had the reputation of being a very devout Christian man, and the offer he presented so surprised her that silence was accepted as encouragement. His hope put a ring in his tone as he informed her that he was preparing to enter the ministry. I cannot recall the young man's name, and know not if he is on earth or in heaven, but I can never forget his look of horror as I exclaimed that I was too frightened to answer him at first; but the information just given settled the matter, for I would never be a minister's wife. He left the house no doubt thanking God for his merciful escape from a girl who could not appreciate the honor.

It may help some one else for me to say that I once had so little reverence that I told the Lord that he was unfair, that it was not right, to lead me to love a man with all my heart, and then call him into the ministry after marriage. But I see now I was very ignorant in those days and saw only the dark side. It is true the trials of a pastor's wife are often sharp and peculiar to the place; but it is just as true, that no other woman can have the exquisite joys that God gives alone to the pastor and his wife.

LIVING WITHIN ONE'S INCOME

IT is said by some that the first three months of a young convert's life will determine his future usefulness. The sweet halo of the winning time is over. The church-members rejoice in possession and begin wisely, or unwisely, to impose burdens on the young Christian and look now to him to help them in winning others. If the burdens and privileges of the new life are accepted in the right spirit there will be growth and development; but if rejected there will come great loss and often utter ruin of all future usefulness.

This crisis comes sooner or later in the home life of every young man and his bride, and as the pastor and his wife are, or should be, an example for all other young people, it is doubly needful that they do not fail. There are ministers today seeking in vain for pastorates, because some time in their lives they failed to adjust their expenses to their incomes, and although repentant, their reputation follows them. God has just given me the power, assisted by others, to very materially aid a pastor, who last year received less than three hundred dollars in cash, and yet saved eleven dollars! This story seems incredible, but I know it to be true. No doubt the fuel and food sent this pastor by his people made his real income larger than that of others whose environments make a larger expenditure seem to be absolutely necessary; but no matter what the demands are, or how small the income, success in the pastorate requires that self-denial shall be exercised until the money received will pay for everything purchased. We do not believe this self-denial should be required only of the wife, and in order that it be equalized it might be a good plan to pay all the general bills and then divide the remainder between the two who should be equally interested. As every one is to give an account of himself to God, the pastor will in this way allow his wife the privilege of being accountable to the church, society, and God for the way in which she divides what is her own.

One large factor in our own happy life has been the account book kept by the pastor since the wedding day. Every day his money is counted before he sleeps and the book shows every penny expended. At the end of the month everything is classified—rent, fuel, food, missions, and charities, and the allowances to each member of the home. This perfect frankness between the pastor and his wife will bring peace to the new home and merry hearts over denials that would otherwise sour and estrange.

One of the charms of courtship was in the constant surprise of the little gifts exchanged. This division of the amount left after the general expenses are paid will make the continuance of this custom possible, and on it much of the happiness of married life depends.

A young pastor we know is soon to marry a lady who has for some years received a very fine salary. We know this pastor's income is very small, but they are both sensible young people, and we cannot believe that this devoted lover will allow his bride's income to cease entirely, and she, in the greater treasure of his love and in her new work, will not sorrow over the luxuries she must lose with her present salary. A long experience proves that happiness does not depend upon a large salary. When a church gives to the pastor all it can, the all may be little, but the hearts of love in it will still find many ways of supplementing the small salary, inexpressibly touching to those who receive. These gifts almost entirely cease in many of our larger churches, so that it was not strange to see a pastor's wife weep when receiving the gift of a Thanksgiving turkey. It reminded her of that little first church of long ago. It is too true, with everything gained there is some loss, and for all those difficult denials of early life in the pastorate there are compensations so sweet that they are never valued until lost in the "greater blessings" we all crave.

In doing right and keeping out of debt we must deny ourselves often much that we enjoyed before marriage; but there is one comfort that can never be taken from the true heart, for ''your Heavenly Father knoweth that ye have need of all these things,'' and if we fulfill the conditions, ''all these things shall be added.''

III

EARNING MONEY

THE question often comes to a pastor's wife: Shall I do anything to earn money? It is a delicate subject, and one that demands serious consideration. There are some who apply the same rule to the wife that they do to the pastor: "Even so hath the Lord ordained that they which preach the gospel should live of the gospel." The disaster that is sure to come to the man who will not abide by the rule may well cause the wife to think twice before she makes a new one for herself. Wisdom teaches that we must count the cost before we begin to build.

Any woman who begins her married life earning money outside of her own home will always be expected to do it, and there will be a sense of loss in the mind of her husband as well as in her own if she does not. The home and church life of a pastor's wife is more taxing than that of the majority of the other women in the church.

The pastor's wife who draws a salary for work she may do throws a searchlight on all her other duties in her home and in the church. Dust or finger marks on the door, or furniture, that would not otherwise be observed, will attain gigantic proportions. Absence from any meeting will be accredited to the outside work, and the refusal to do anything, no matter how unjust the request, will have the same motive applied. If the home and church work of a pastor's wife is all she can do well, does it not naturally follow that it is not best to shorten one's life by any burden that is needless?

"Needless!" I hear as a united exclamation from many voices, "you know nothing about it." But I do. My husband's first salary as a pastor was ten dollars a week, in the suburb of one of our largest cities. The ladies in the city churches overestimated my talents, and brought me into a prominence that taxed my slender resources to the utmost. My husband is now pastor of a large city church where the salary might look large to many who have less, but I can say truthfully, we are just as poor now as we were then, and the reasons are two-fold.

A small church will rally around a pastor's family as a large one will not. I recall with pleasure a dressmaker in that little church who made my gowns without charge, and another lady who had been a tailoress in her youth, as beautiful work on my children's clothes testified, gave substantial aid. No such assistance comes in a large church; and in such a church the demands upon the purse of the pastor are a hundred-fold greater. The charity work sometimes falls entirely upon his shoulders, so that large and small churches can unite in the same prayer: ''Lord, keep him humble, and we will keep him poor.''

There is occasionally found in a church some lady who appreciates the work of the pastor's wife. She sees that the extra work put into the church would realize for her as a teacher or in some other vocation a handsome salary and much leisure, and this observant Christian makes her appreciation practical. It has been my good fortune to find in all these years one such woman. She is very wealthy and is an invalid, and with my superb health I have been hands and feet for her among the sick and desolate. In these years she has given me many dollars. If there were such women in every church the burden of the pastor's wife would be lifted, and she could sing, instead of sighing, her way into heaven.

No useful talent should be neglected, no matter if the searchlights of the world should be drawn upon it, but never let the world pay you for something you would not do for it without recompense. Better write for the Christian press under your own name, than for money, what you would blush to have your friends know to be yours.

Perhaps you have left the life of a successful teacher to cast in your lot with a poor theologian. Do your very best work in the Sunday-school, and if he has neither time nor inclination for indoctrinating the young people, do not leave it undone through your neglect.

Whatever your peculiar talent, let it shine

for Christ. If you can cultivate it quietly at home while other women are doing fancy work, looking out of the window, or aimlessly tossing over drygoods, so much the better for you and the church. If it brings you money, it is their gain as well as yours. Ere long the church and the whole Christian world will wake up to an appreciation of their own, and while they do good to all men it will be especially to the household of faith.

IV

THE GIFT OF SILENCE

ONE of the doctrines of the Roman Catholic Church, the celibacy of the priesthood, is founded on the supposition that a wife cannot control her tongue. We do not say this is the only excuse for the doctrine in the Roman Church, but it is one of them. In our so-called Protestant churches there is often the gravest necessity for a pastor's wife to exercise the golden gift of silence, and we rejoice that so large a majority are not found wanting when weighed in the balances.

Sometimes a pastor assumes that his wife cannot be trusted with the knowledge in hand. This we believe to be a great mistake on his part. Unless his wife is insane or idiotic she is worthy of trust. From the very nature of affairs she must know something of every subject that can come under consideration, and knowing all she is less apt to make a blunder than she would be to know but a part. The object of this writing is to urge upon the wives of pastors to cultivate to the highest degree the power of being trusted not only by their husbands but by others.

Often silly children go about among their playmates with the boast "I know a secret but I won't tell you." It is possible for a pastor's wife to allow the confidence given her to lie as near the surface and her manner say as plainly as words, "I know something you don't know." Eyes as well as tongues must be under complete control.

Children should be trained in the home from their earliest years not to tell everything they know. They should be taught to say to one who pries too closely: "I would rather you would ask father or mother about it."

But suppose one had not been trained in childhood to control the tongue. The case is not hopeless. Experience is a costly teacher but she is a good one, and if a mistake has been made let the pastor and his wife look it bravely in the face.

Be patient and helpful with each other and progress will be made. Sometimes the very best pastor and one who is the truest and most devoted husband, will assume when a criticism is made that his wife is to blame, just as he would, in his humility, assume that he was to blame if the criticism had been made upon himself. Never let a wife be depressed if blamed unjustly —a judicious patient silence will generally bring everything around all right.

We remember with the profoundest gratitude the pastor's wife of our girlhood. Into her ear was poured all our love affairs and our ambition for an education, and it was through her influence that we were given the very best opportunities at home and abroad. In the love affairs we did not then see her guiding hand and it was all the stronger that we did not see it— and by the way there is just where the power of a husband or wife lies in guiding without the other knowing it.

A good pastor's wife and a pastor's good wife will not need to go about seeking the confidence of people. She will draw those who need such help as surely as a magnet draws. No matter how highly gifted a pastor's wife may be by education and natural endowments, she must always remember that she is the pastor's wife and not the pastor. A pastor's confidence in his wife is certainly misplaced if it causes her to assume the lead or in any way insist that her opinion on a subject shall be preferred to the pastor's.

No matter how utterly the pastor confides in his wife or how worthy she is of his confidence, she is in the pew and he is in the pulpit, and for this very reason she can be of the utmost use to her husband.

The ideal church prays for its pastor, bears his burdens, and lifts him up to his own ideal and its for him, although all churches do not fulfill their mission. But no pastor need despair who has down in in the pew a noble, true-hearted wife who is working and praying for him; and let him remember that "a little leaven leaveneth the whole lump."

V

LEADING CONTRIBUTORS

PASTORS' wives should be leading contributors in the churches of which they are members, not only to the missionary and charitable societies but to church finances, including their husbands' salaries. We may not be able to give the largest amount each week, or month—according as the custom of the church may be—but we can give the largest proportion of our income.

The old-time idea that the pastor is an object of charity has passed away even in the most benighted regions. This fact is due largely to our religious press. There are countless other transformations due to this same agency, if we had but patience to make a study of the facts.

Between the very few who are still mendicants, and the number who give cheerfully "as the Lord hath prospered," we have the great majority of pastors' wives. Somebody must lead in this ideal effort now before the religious world. Who can do it better than we?

We were once fortunate enough to be members of a church where the rule recorded on the books was "that every member of the church should either contribute to the support of the church or be supported by the church." This rule was a good one as far as it went. We would have added: " Those supported by the church must return a proportion as their own contribution."

This ideal rule was interpreted in a peculiar way. When we offered what they considered a generous subscription, we were told that we were supported by the church and were thus exempt. The freedom offered was neither appreciated nor accepted. We replied that our husband's salary was earned, and should be paid as the salaries of their school teachers were paid, and that we were under as much obligation to the church and to God to contribute to the expenses of the church as the teachers or any one else in the church.

They acknowledged that we had the better of the argument, and during a long pastorate we gave with joy as we had received. We have not been a single day without a salary in all these years, and we count that the promise has been fulfilled, " Give and it shall be given," etc.

The testimony of countless pastors' wives could be given to prove the joy and healthful influence of this systematic giving by pastors' families; for our work is not done unless all under our roof share in this duty. My Protestant cook may have more money in the bank than I shall ever have, and if she is a church-member or a regular attendant, it is mine to influence her to generous giving. I may only be permitted to give my hundreds; a child in my home may yet be able to give his thousands and tens of thousands. Will he look back and bless me that his first thought and love of giving came from my precept and example?

If your own experience does not echo the thought, will you not try it just as you would accept from me a new pattern for a garment, or a recipe for cooking? If you do not feel that you owe it to your church or to your denomination, will you not acknowledge that you do owe it to your God, and do it heartily unto him if not unto men?

VI

HOLDING OFFICE

SOME of the most important things a pastor's wife can do are the most difficult to describe. In some way she should always be found among the soul winners in the church. In order to have the strength and time for this most important work, it would be well to accept as few official positions as possible.

It is the custom when a new pastor comes to the church to offer his wife the presidency of the Ladies' Society or societies. I can think of many reasons why she should not accept these tender overtures of love and honor.

There are in every church, no matter how small, women who are by nature fitted for these offices and the ideal pastor's wife should delight in the discovery of such workers, and she will be longer and better loved for helping to train such women than if she filled the office herself. Again, the most successful pastors are those who can leave a church in the best running order, and his wife should so regulate her work that their leaving should jar as few interests as possible. But the most important reason for not accepting these offices is that both the time and attention they absorb are too much for any pastor's wife who has before her the aspiration of being the very best she possibly can be.

Twice only, and then under the strongest protest, have I accepted the presidency of any existing society I found on coming to a church. The first time it was on the condition that I be released at the end of the year if I found a woman to take my place. I found the woman and so impressed my thought upon the members that I think no pastor's wife has since been president of the society. The second time, I found upon coming to an old and influential church that a lady had been president of one of the missionary societies for a number of years. Her influence with the ladies was so great that once again I was overpowered and became president " for one year only.'' Of course I had pride enough to do my best, and the money given that year was more than any previous year, but after a year's rest this lady so eminently fitted for the office was induced to take it again.

There are doubtless exceptions to all rules but a good general one to have, taught me by experience and a wide observation, is that to be a teacher in the Sunday-school and a member of the Sunday-school Library Committee are all the offices a pastor's wife ought to accept. This rule should not apply to new work in the church that a wide-awake pastor sees ought to be taken up.

It may then seem absolutely necessary for a pastor's wife to come into prominence, but even then she should in her own mind be on the keenest search for some one to take her place.

It has been my fortune or misfortune, according to the standpoint from which it is viewed, to inaugurate various enterprises in churches where we have worked, but God has always helped me to leave them in better hands than my own, so that frequent and constant reports of the work often cheer me over some present difficulty. We should continually shrink from prominence, but not from work or influence.

VII

MAKING CHANGES

THE ideal way for a young pastor to begin his work is with a newly organized church. Then pastor and people can experiment and together evolve the best methods of church work. In this evolution no doubt mistakes will be made, but they will be mutual and all will see the funny side and laugh them off, just as the blunders of early housekeeping and the training of the first baby will convulse those most interested when experience comes to enlighten.

How well I remember leaning over our first baby, watching her as she smiled in her sleep! The nurse was deaf and did not hear our words, but noting the seraphic expression of our countenances, she guessed our meaning and enlightened us with a laconic, "Wind!" It has been a little watchword with us since.

If a young pastor cannot begin with a new church, let him do the next best thing and take a small church. There are many reasons for doing this that he cannot fully appreciate at first, but they will grow upon him as he adjusts himself to his new life. The pastor's wife will find the training of her experience in a small church just what she will need when her pastor is called to a larger field of usefulness, as he no doubt will be, if he is faithful in the small one and keeps himself growing all the time. If any one rule has insured our present success, it has been our determination to be our best at all times. No sermon or testimony has ever been withheld or saved for a larger or better audience. The few who dared venture in the storm came the next time, for they knew they received the very best the preacher could give them. The deep and rich experience, the knitting together of the very souls of pastor and people that is known only by those who experiment together until the times and methods of doing work are fixed, are so sweet and peculiar that one hesitates to analyze them. Such a pastor may have a very marked success in his first church and fail in his second, because from the first he cannot conceal the fact that he is chilled and handicapped by the methods of work. It is to the wife of such a pastor I want to whisper words of hope and comfort, for it is yours to strengthen and encourage. Draw the pastor's mind from methods to the people, for he must needs know them well before he attempts radical changes. Though he himself may survive a rash movement on his part, the church may be divided and he have to leave ruin where he found only harmony.

Perhaps the method of raising money by pew rentals is as dear to the church as the apple of its eye, and the pastor is an enthusiast for free pews and voluntary subscriptions; or perhaps the pastor does not care particularly how it is raised, but he is very sure the church has the wrong men in office, or that the Sunday-school, which is held in the afternoon, should immediately follow the morning service. The pastor is not always right on these questions, for what is a success in one church cannot perhaps be in another, and there are always

two sides to every question. *E. g.*, the
school at the noon hour would accommo-
date those who live at a distance from the
church and those who want the afternoon
for reading and sleep, or it may be the
time is wanted for mission work; on the
other hand, when the school follows the
morning service, the members are shut off
from their social hour, which is invaluable.
Then there are busy women who could not
come to morning services without depriving
some one of the school.

But there are other things about which
there is not a question, and just here comes
the supreme test to the patience of the
pastor and his wife. Don't move too
soon! Perhaps as the mistake, or evil it
may be, bursts upon your vision, you may
feel that you have come to the kingdom
for just such a time as this; but remember
how slowly and cautiously the queen
worked. If you are right, you are a
"worker together with God." Don't
move any faster than he does. The prime
object in coming to the church was to feed
the sheep and lambs and convert the sinner
from the error of his way. If you have

been faithful to these, and there has been time for a deep confidence in you to grow in the hearts of the people, they will listen more readily to the proposed changes. It is in such crises as these that the power of the pastor's wife is felt. If she will drink long and deeply every morning of the spiritual medicine,—one-half dove, one-half serpent,—then if it is right for the changes to come, they will come, or, what may be just as well, success will come in spite of the methods.

VIII

GIVING PRAISE

IF your husband is to be a successful
pastor, you must not fail to give him
frequent and tender praise when he has
done his best. Do not be so ready with
your criticism. If he knows he has failed,
there is no use of "rubbing it in," and if
he does not know it, and you have been
wise and faithful in your words of praise,
their absence will be all he will require.

A pastor needs a good wife more than
any other man, for his occupation is not
one in which he can forget his sorrow or
chagrin; he cannot, like the worldly man,
smoke it away in the club or drink it off in
the saloon. There are delightful women
who, from girlhood, devote all their ener-
gies to their husbands' interests, but they
neglect this one little habit of praise. A
second wife, who has it, takes her place
when she has fallen to enjoy the man and

the fortune her heroic efforts have made, and we are regaled with such sentences as the following, found in the review of a recent Sunday-school lesson: "A husband may lose his wife by death and marry another wife who may be even dearer to him than the first." We think the writer went "a long way around" to lug this sentence into that particular Sunday-school lesson, but he or she gave me a good text. We, as pastors' wives, ought not to wear ourselves out and thus give place to a second; and if in spite of all our care we must go first, let us be so lovely and lovable that no second wife can ever be dearer.

But there are some pastors that no wife could keep from disaster. I recall one who came to our home on his wedding tour. In a whisper we foretold for the queenly, intellectual bride an early death in her efforts to "keep up" with her husband as he hurried her breathlessly hither and thither; but we were mistaken. She has survived the wear and tear *physically*, and they are the parents of children any one might envy; but where has the trouble been that his pastorates have been short and unsatisfactory? A very foolish little reason some would say. He was not content to fly on the wing of love into every home in his parish, sing his song of hope and go, but instead, he was content to be caged by a few women who flattered him. They knew not how to truly praise. "One made a chicken pie he loved." She made it often and he went to eat it. "One talked so respectfully of religion," and he went to listen; another always wanted "to consult about something." And the wife, what shall we say of her? Only this: a part of his punishment is that she has learned for herself a little of the lesson he has been so many years in teaching her, unconsciously, by his own example. But let us all hope they have seen their danger in time and have yet a glorious future before them.

Let us, as pastors' wives, make our home cages so large, so delightful, that the one we love will not *feel* the bars, but will always be more than glad to return.

IX

THE PASTOR'S STUDY

MY own experience, and that of many others with whom I have conferred, convinces me that the best place for a pastor's study is in his own home.

Our pastor's first study was in the church. We did not realize until the books were taken from the house how much we should miss them, but thinking it only a part of the self-denial required of pastors' wives we did not dream of complaining. Ere long, however, the pastor missed them. Some, which he valued and was not able to replace, went away never to return; some of them he loaned; and others were borrowed without permission. He is possessed of boundless patience, but he lost a small fraction of it when one of his deacons rested the window on his precious Inter-leaved Bible, and a rain coming in the night ruined the work of several years.

When the pastor, at home, is bored with a tedious caller the cook can do a little to keep the dinner from spoiling, but who can describe the suspense and delay when the pastor is pinned down in the church study with no one to help him? There are many other good reasons for not having the study in the church that will readily occur to the mind of any thoughtful person.

The study in the home should be the most pleasant room in the house. It is not right to give to the guest who may sleep once in your home the choice room and to your pastor one that is small, poorly ventilated, or in any way unattractive. To be sure, sometimes this idea is carried too far. We know one pastor who is a source of amusement for all who know him. He has the front parlor for his study and in the evening his curtains are not drawn, and people in the city drive past the house to see the pastor "posing." They are not troubled for the want of room and have no children, so that there is no excuse for this nonsense; but there are more pastors' wives who err in the other extreme. This subject came up in conversation when away on our vacation, and the wife of a city pastor said she could hardly wait to go home, she was so anxious to give her pastor the guest room he had so long wanted for his study.

The pastor's wife should take the entire charge of the study. Experience will soon teach her how to dust and put everything back in its place, and how to ventilate when the room is to be left only a short time. The location of the study, its furnishings, its ventilation, and other care necessary, has more to do with the quality of the pastor's sermons than the inexperienced would imagine.

The pastor once in the pleasant study is not all. Let the wife guard him from all possible interruption. This task will be very difficult in the first year of a pastorate, but as the people learn to appreciate the need of uninterrupted study they will find that the devoted pastor's wife can answer many questions and attend to a multitude of callers that would otherwise spoil a sermon. Most of all, let the pastor's wife keep out of the study during sermon-making hours. There are times when no human friend except the divine Elder Brother is appreciated by the pastor. When the pastor and his wife are entirely one in the work, this is sometimes a very difficult restraint for the wife to put upon herself, but the best success in life makes it absolutely necessary. It is difficult to always remember to replace a book you have taken from its shelf and to train the children to regard the sanctity of the pastor's retreat; but "practice" will in time make "perfect."

X

HOME RELIGION

THERE is no one more responsible for the depth and purity of home religion than the pastor's wife. Very little things will break the regularity and interest in family worship, which is the very foundation of home religion. No uniform method can be suggested or adopted, because circumstances vary. In our family we have worship twice every day. In the morning before we leave the breakfast table the pastor reads the Scripture selected in course for reading the Bible entire in a prescribed time. The reading is followed by prayer, which always closes with the Lord's prayer, in which all unite. Before retiring the pastor and his wife together pour out their hearts in prayer for many blessings that could not so well be specified before others. Where the entire family are interested in the Sunday-school the discussion of points in the lesson are often very helpful for all. But the wife who is much alone with God will not lack for opportunities. Our Heavenly Father is very indulgent. He comes and talks with us while our needles hurry in and out of the tasks which are often heavier than we can bear. Often in city life he is the only guest to whom we can say: "Please excuse me if I work while we talk."

If our own home religion is pure and natural we will find ere long that we are influencing other homes. A pastor's wife should go with her husband to every funeral where he officiates, unless there is a good reason for her not going. It has always been my habit to call, after the funeral, with the pastor, and I have always found that my self-denial in going has been the surest entrance into the hearts and homes. When grief has made the hearts tender, then experienced tact knows how to take advantage. I shall never forget the dismal wail of an old woman upon whom we once called, who said her "time was past." "It is too late for me to be saved." "When my husband died, I thought Christian people would come and ask me to come to Jesus. Oh, I was ripe for it then! But they never came. Oh, I was ripe for it then! Now it is too late.''

Our custom is when we go to a church to at once obtain a list of the '' shut-ins '' and together we call on them as soon as possible. While we are doing this, the ladies who are able to make calls come to see me. These calls I return as soon as I have finished the others. A pastor's wife should study the church list, and if after some time she finds that a lady has not called on her, she should waive the usual rule and call upon the delinquent.

There can be no fixed rule about praying in the homes visited; every pastor must make his own rule. Often he is asked and then, of course, the way is plain. Blessed are the pastor and his wife who enjoy granting the request.

Sometimes a home seems shut and barred against all religious influences. I recall a neighbor and his wife who had two lovely little children. All the advances that could be thought of were made, apparently without effect. One morning our door bell rang violently, and an excited messenger called to me to come quickly. "Mrs. —— had sent her. The child— the baby boy—was dying!" I was there in a moment. The child had been taking his late breakfast of bread and milk, and had seemed to choke and not to regain his breath. I held him upright in my arms and set every one to work. In a few moments I had him in a warm bath, always holding him so that his lungs had full play. I wrapped him in warm blankets and tried artificial respiration. One of the messengers finally succeeded in finding a physician who could not believe the child was dead until he had applied every known test. He approved what I had done, and there was never any lack of feeling on the part of the parents after that. They were not even members of our congregation, but they were our neighbors, and as such we were in a degree responsible.

The command to rejoice with those who rejoice is as binding as the one to weep with the sorrowful. So that the pastor's wife is welcomed at the weddings. Even if she is not invited, she has a right to go

and her lack of invitation is always an over-
sight or from ignorance, which it is her
duty to forgive and overlook. I used to
have all the wedding fees, but they were
borrowed, and soon even that ceremony
was dispensed with ; but I have such an
interest in the general fund that I can generally capture all the weddings that come
near enough.

I try to know the pastor's engagements,
and when the shy young fellow is about to
turn away disappointed because the pastor
is not in, I ask him if it is a wedding, and
very seldom do I make a mistake. He
tells me the time and place, which I carefully record. Then I tell him the pastor
gives a beautiful certificate, and if he is
sure the names are all right in the license,
and will leave it with me, the certificate can
be filled. If the pastor has an imperative
engagement and the gentleman will not
change the hour, I can help him to get
some one else if he has no choice. A little
kindness and tact on the part of the pastor's wife insures her many marriages in
her own parlor, which should always have
a welcome for those who need it. Hearts

are as easily won in joy as in sorrow, and if a woman has no higher ambition than to be popular, it is a greater honor to reign in the hearts and homes of the great majority than to be queen in some narrow society circle.

XI

THE SUNDAY-SCHOOL AND RELIGIOUS JOURNAL

A THOROUGH acquaintance with the church and congregation is a great advantage to a pastor in his work. One very good way to accomplish this is for the pastor and his wife to act as supply teachers in the Sunday-school. There may be good reasons why a pastor's wife cannot become a permanent teacher in the school, but there are few who cannot prepare the lesson each week and be present in the school. If all the teachers are present, a good opportunity will then be had to visit the different departments or sit on a back seat and overlook the school. The writer is blessed with such vigorous health that she is able to teach an adult Bible class in the audience room at noon and act as supply teacher in the school at 2.30; but so impressed is she with the value of knowing the entire school, that if one must be given up, it would be the regular class.

The acquaintance with the girls and boys thus gained must be experienced to be appreciated. A large part of many city schools is composed of children whose parents do not attend church. This supply teaching is the entrance wedge into such homes and untold good is accomplished. If the pastor's wife will attend the teachers' meeting, she will come into yet closer sympathy with the teachers and school.

There are some things a pastor's wife can do better than any one else simply because she *is* the pastor's wife. One of these things we believe to be the circulation and increased subscription of our denominational newspapers.

She may have no talent and very little opportunity for other work in the church, but we can think of nothing that could prevent her from doing this service for the Master. Even if confined to an invalid's chair or bed, it need not limit the opportunity for this work. A pastor's wife too ill to call upon others seldom lacks for calls herself. Sample copies of the paper are always ready for those who will use them wisely. A long experience has taught us that these should not be distributed at random. Read the paper carefully; mark what you think will interest the non-subscriber you give or send the paper to. Do not take a refusal as a final "No." Reply kindly that if it is not convenient to subscribe now, it may be later, and ask that you may be notified when it is. If you do not hear in a few months, try again. Our experience might furnish many illustrations of how successful work has been done, but we believe one's own experience, as costing more, is better appreciated. There are very few pastors who do not soon learn the value of the paper to themselves and congregations. They are too busy to do much about getting subscribers, and one who does not value the paper has very little influence in interesting others.

If pastors' wives all along the line would join hands in this good work, we would see glorious results. We will not leave it for the editor to say that the writer of this is not his wife, and will add that we have in several cities lived under the shadow of influential Baptist newspapers, and "ye editors" would testify, if called upon, that we have practised, and are practising, much better than we have preached.

XII

DECLINING A MOLD

IT sometimes occurs that the very best thing a pastor's wife can do is to say " No."

Always refuse to be pressed into the mold of some former pastor's wife. This must be done with the utmost kindness and wisdom so that no offense can be taken. It is natural for us to love old people, and we enjoy ministering to their comfort, so that we were surprised once at a little cloud that seemed to come between us and the older ladies in a city church of which we had become members. At last it was explained. The former pastor had been an old man; he and his lovely wife were without children and without any ambition for church extension that would consume time or energy, and the dear old ladies had been in the habit of spending the day at the parsonage whenever it pleased them to do so. Finding the new pastor's wife out hunting up new people, or entertaining many important callers in an hour, was something so unexpected and disagreeable that for a time it did not seem to them they could endure it. Born with a wonderful love of *time*, and having that love cultivated by the best of teachers, it was some time before we understood. Even then we did not "let on," but by every art known to us we won those dear old ladies into loving us and into sympathy with our plans, and in a few years we had no better friends.

If you rebel against the work forced upon you, do not let any one suspect it. Do the best you can, and God will either remove the thorn or give you grace to bear it. We know the wife of a man rarely gifted as a pastor. He left his pastorate because his wife would not make a few calls. It was not the failure to make the calls that caused the trouble, but *her talk about it*. We are not of so much consequence in the world as we think we are when we do right, and the calls would probably have not been missed if she had not boasted that she would not make them.

It is cruel to marry a pastor without love for his work or at least without a desire to grow into a love for it; but loving and trusting him, and loving his work, all things are possible.

XIII

ON BAPTISM

THE way in which a pastor administers the ordinances will very largely affect his success. The pastor's wife may often suggest improvements in these methods.

If she is a soul winner, it will seem natural for her to be present when ladies come before the examining committee. If there is no committee and the candidates come immediately before the church, the pastor's wife can be present when the pastor instructs those who are to be baptized. A baptism loses much of its beauty and solemnity because those who are to be baptized are not told beforehand what they are expected to do.

We know an overworked pastor who is often called into other churches to baptize their candidates during the illness or absence of the regular pastor. This minister's only skill lies in the fact that he calmly and carefully explains every step to be taken. It is done in this way: "There are five steps down into the baptistery; when you reach the last one I will tell you, and I will take both of your hands in mine in this way (his wife folds her hands one over the other and the minister takes both in his left hand to show just how he will do it); I do so because, if I did not, you would be apt to throw one or both of your hands up when I baptized you. We will walk well into the baptistery, and when we stop I will ask you the question: 'Do you believe that Jesus Christ is the Son of God and your Saviour?' You must answer: 'I do,' in a clear voice. Then I will say: 'Oh this confession of your faith I baptize thee in the name of the Father and of the Son and of the Holy Ghost. Amen.' While I am repeating this formula, I want you to close your eyes and your lips and stop breathing; don't catch your breath but simply stop breathing—so." And he shows how it is done. In his own church the attendants never fail to shake out the handkerchief of each candidate as he goes down, and it is handed to the candidate with the admonition to "give it to the pastor," who tucks it in the folds of his own robe, and it is there, dry, and in a convenient form to be used to wipe the water from the face after baptism.

These seem to be trifling matters, but without them the timid will be confused, and others will, without thought, do little things that will detract much from the solemnity of the act. The baptismal robes should be made with a wide box plait down the center of the back. This gives the best help possible for a beautiful baptism, when it is explained to the candidate that he must neither resist nor in any way attempt to assist the administrator by throwing himself backward. Intelligent school children know how much lighter a weight is in water, and that the feet of the candidate may be firmly planted on the floor of the baptistery during the baptism, for all the minister has to do is to draw, not push, the head and shoulders of the candidate under the water.

It often falls to the lot of the pastor's wife to remind even intelligent people that if the water in the baptistery were not warmed to correspond with the temperature of the room, it would chill the candidate and administrator more than a baptism in the open air. A warm-hearted, intelligent, sympathetic patience will accomplish much. If it is in her heart, let her whisper to those who are to be baptized: "Do not look around the room or seem to see any one in the audience; look straight forward until you close your eyes; then, with a prayer in your heart that God will so help you to honor him that some one else will be led to follow Christ in baptism, commit your way to him, and remember I am praying for you."

XIV

ON COMMUNION

WE have sometimes thought that the deacon who has charge of the communion service, and his good wife who so faithfully does her share of the work every month, can enter more fully into sympathy with the pastor than those Christians who have no such responsibility.

A tender word of appreciation from the pastor's wife, her word of inquiry or regret when one is absent, can do much to make the service what it should be—a solemn spiritual feast for the soul. The wise pastor will give his message in the sermon that precedes the communion service, and if he must share with some "visiting brother," he will give him the wine to pour and ask him to pray. Years since, when we came home from our first communion served by our present pastor, we exclaimed with tears, "Thank you for that blessed service."

"What was there peculiar about it?" he asked. "Oh, you did not talk, you let the Saviour give the message." "Oh," he replied, "I did not talk because I had nothing to say." "God grant you never may," I exclaimed with emphasis. And he never has.

If the pastor or his people wish to see the bread broken, a finger bowl and napkin should be included in the service, and the pastor must not fail to use it. It can be done so quietly and naturally that the act will scarcely be noticed. The one who prepares the bread should cut it into small squares so that it will come apart easily. The most beautiful and impressive way to serve the bread is for each one to wait until all are served. Then let the pastor, with the bread in his hand, say, "Eat ye all of it." We have not seen the individual communion cups used, but we should think where they are used, it would add to the service to repeat, "Drink ye all of it."

We believe most emphatically in the unfermented wine, or in the fermented with the ferment taken out by a patented process. We used it in one church and it was

universally liked. We now use the unfermented and no reformed drunkard is
tempted with it.

If the "Poor Fund" is low, or there
is a special need, a word from the pastor
will be one "fitly spoken," and if gold
coins rest on the silver communion plate,
would the quotation not be completed?

While we do not believe that the bread
and wine is the real body and blood of
Christ any more truly than that he is a
"door" or a "vine," for he was alive
when he said that it was his body, still we
must not go to the other extreme and
neglect or fail to appreciate the worth of
the communion service. If I had the pen
of the poet, I would picture the pastor
earnest and true, the seven deacons, "un-
spotted from the world, visiting the widow
and fatherless in their affliction," the great
rank and file of faithful ones, who think no
denial too great to come to the church to
"show the Lord's death till he come." Then
shall be that last great supper where we, his
honored guests, shall see him in person.
The deacons' and pastors' wives who are
faithful here will not be forgotten there.

XV

RELATIVE TO OTHER PASTORS' WIVES

THE fact that pastors' wives are not organized into a society is no reason why they should not exert a world-wide influence over each other. Let this influence begin in your own city. If your hear a vacant church near you is to have a new pastor, send to his wife a letter of welcome. The writer has received such letters and values them highly. If possible, follow the letter with a call as soon as you know it will be convenient. There is no obligation to repeat the calls, for one's own church will give about all the calling any ordinary woman can do, but other kindly acts will be suggested to the mind that is intent on doing favors.

Perhaps you keep a carriage and the new acquaintance does not. A ride to some meeting together is appreciated. No rule can be given. "Circumstances alter cases." If you cannot invite to your own home, you certainly can to a social or entertainment in your church. Of course, this kindness is sometimes misplaced, and the one so lovingly welcomed repays you by stealing your members or something equally bad; but better this nine times over than that one loyal, true heart should be overlooked and left to loneliness.

I have not space or time to enlarge this thought, but if you have not realized this obligation to other pastors' wives, the thought will grow in your own minds and you will no doubt do more beautiful things than I have ever imagined.

There is delicious work we can do for the wives of our home missionaries. If you are loved and trusted in your church, the ladies will bring you their best to fill a barrel. We remember once, a few months after removing to a city church, asking for material for a box, and so generous was the response that we filled nine; in every one was a winter wrap, a shawl, and a waterproof. Some ladies are afraid of the criticism of the church ladies, but have no such fear of the pastor's wife. Of course

E

we know this is hard work; but my mother used to say, ''Anything well done is hard work,'' even being lazy.

Our foreign missionaries must not be forgotten. A dainty handkerchief tucked in a loving letter, a new book, a tray cioth, any little gift, will brighten their Christmas. It should be sent early to reach them in time. We don't need organization. The atmosphere is not organized, though I verily believe there are people who would capture it if they could and make us pay dearly for it. With our gifts and our prayers for each other, who can foretell what God will accomplish through us?

XVI

ALABASTER BOXES

THE world has been perfumed many times since Mary broke the alabaster box, and no one has greater influence in repeating the service than the wives of the pastors.

Society has countless tender courtesies that are ignored by too many church-members, and it is for the pastor's wife to be "as wise in her generation as the world." Her writing desk must never be without acceptance stationery and every invitation must be answered promptly. When the lady who was obliged to leave her card is next seen, do not fail to offer her your verbal regrets. These thoughtful attentions must not cease in sending written acceptance or regrets for formal invitations, but if the pastor's wife has failed to attend a social or missionary meeting, she should in some way communicate with those who had the meeting in charge. In a city church these obligations so multiply that a confirmed invalid must needs be excused, but even an invalid can send from her sick-room messages that will brighten and sweeten this old world of ours. Our religious papers are filled with beautiful poems and stories. The pastor's wife can cut these out before the papers are destroyed and paste them on bright cards or colored paper, and the planning where to give or send them brings a bit of romance into the dreariest life. If the pastor's wife has a loving heart and is always polite and courteous, the pastor has the best illustration at hand for anything he may say on the subject. In fact, in these matters example is better than precept.

Just how and when the pastor's family shall entertain is a difficult question to decide. We remember when our work was in a church so small that we entertained, in instalments, all the church-members at tea ; but our experience has been that too much can be done for a church, so that the members will leave most of the work of this kind for the pastor's wife to do. But the effect of not doing enough is almost as serious

A very pleasant way is to throw the parsonage open from three to six in the afternoon and from eight until eleven the same evening. The refreshments can be inexpensive, but should be daintily served in the dining room. We have several times entertained the deacons and their wives at dinner, and occasionally the compliment has been returned. When small companies are entertained at the pastor's, there should be some good reason for it. The Sunday-school classes of the pastor and his wife, the ushers, or some sharp division should be made, so that no one can be offended. When a pastor changes from one church to another, he should not be in haste to entertain his people in his own home. Let time decide for him the tastes and customs of his people, and then he will not have to regret burdens assumed that are neither enjoyed nor appreciated. Some pastors find it possible to have one evening "at home" in each week. If his people bring strangers to his house, it is well worth the sacrifice, but when the church-members do not call on that evening more than on any other, and the pastor frequently accepts other invitations and leaves the burden of entertaining on his wife, then she has a right to request a change.

The wives of some pastors never know when a guest may materialize. This is a mistake. The pastor is not required to ask every man who happens to call about meal-time to stay; if he does, he will soon have more than he can endure. It is like feeding too many tramps. They mark the house.

The only question that need trouble the pastor's wife is to know that she has the spirit and heart for bringing joy to those about her and the judgment to control her impulses. A good rule is, not to so exhaust ourselves in one department of work that we are unfit to enjoy others. We can easily see what holds society together—a certain charm of person and manner that no doubt often requires an effort. But should we do less for Christ? Can we expect success if we are cold and selfish? Suppose others seem so to us. You remember the old story of the wind and the sun.

We were in a church five years once before we saw much response, but there is a soft place in every heart, and time and persistent effort will find it. Is it fair to carry a sad face to the rank and file of your congregation because a few think you too cheerful and undertake to discipline you? There is only one way for us to keep sweet, and that is, to do our work heartily as unto God and not unto men. Mary no doubt made denials in accumulating money for the purchase of the alabaster box. Denials will give to us the power to brighten many lives, and in giving joy to others our own hearts will overflow.

XVII

OUR HOMES AND OUR INTIMATE FRIENDS

THERE are two luxuries denied the successful pastor and his wife. One is a home, and the other is intimate friends among their parishioners. To some natures these blessings do not seem luxuries, but rather absolute necessities. The love of home is inbred in some hearts and cultivated through life, so that the frequent migrations of the pastorate are a source of terror and abject misery. In my own case I had lived from childhood until marriage in one home, and so had my ancestors before me lived long years in their old homesteads, so that I have often thought the physical act of dying could have no more pain for me than the removals from one house to another. Some churches love their neighbors as they do themselves, and are careful to provide comfortable parsonages for their pastors. If a pastor finds such a church home awaiting him, it in some degree compensates the loss of a house that is absolutely his own.

If a pastor does not find a parsonage, but is afterward able to influence the building of one, it is his duty to see that it is made as convenient for his wife as possible. It is not best to connect the parsonage with the church. It would be just as sensible for a merchant to unite his residence with his store; but a parsonage on the church lot is better than none.

Every minister's home should have a small reception room, with furniture that cannot be easily injured in stormy weather, and where the tedious caller cannot interfere with others. If such a room is available, children can more frequently be invited, and they will feel more inclined to come if they are in no danger of doing injury to the delicate appointments of the house.

The giving up of intimate friends may seem to some an irreparable loss, but it has many compensations. A pastor and his wife who are faithful to all their members have little time or nerve left for intimate friends. These intimacies, which seem so pleasant, often become burdensome, and in the pastorate absolutely dangerous, for we may guard our tongues ever so carefully, and there may be no breath of slander in our words, yet we may be suspected of confidences we had no thought of making, and harm will come.

There is a compensation when a pastor removes from one field to another. Then he and his wife are free to receive into their homes and hearts some faithful one in their former pastorate. I find it valuable as well as extremely pleasant to have one correspondent in every former church home. From them I can hear of the conversions for which we prayed while with them, and bearing each other's burdens they become lighter.

There are exceptions to all rules, and it may be that some pastors have been enabled to purchase homes of their own and to live happily in them for a term of years; but these exceptions are so rare that it will not be safe to depend upon them as examples. It may also be true that some pastor's wife has been able to have an intimate friend without realizing any loss to herself or the church, but I have not known of any one who has been able to do it; on the other hand, I have known of much evil resulting from disregarding the law. Every pastor and his wife are accountable to God if they do not do all they can for the general uplifting of the church which they serve, and in doing this the desire for special friendships will be absorbed and the gratitude of many will fill their hearts to overflowing.

While writing this paper, a young lady came on an errand. She is the only child of rich and influential parents; but, as she told me, "They care nothing for social life"; I invited her in and exerted myself to entertain her, and not in vain, for she enjoyed the call. There was more real pleasure to both of us than there would have been to two who "were always running into each other's homes," often unexpected, and also sometimes unwelcome.

In some churches there is a fund left by will for a parsonage. There is such a one in our present church, but it cannot be used until enough is added to purchase or build a parsonage. Now, it is the pastor's duty to provoke his church to every good word and work, and often in the bringing about of some material good to a church a spiritual blessing follows. But if there is one pastor's wife who must go through life without an earthly home, be assured that to her there will be a larger welcome and a more abundant entrance into her "mansion" that is awaiting her among the "many."

XVIII

THE PASTOR'S WIFE A WIDOW

THIS may be after a short pastorate in one church. It may be after long ones in many churches. It may be by accident. It may be by some disease common to all men. It may be from a broken heart. No matter how it comes, the manner of its coming is swallowed up in the awful fact that the pastor's wife is a widow. The first great shock has passed; the painful excitement of the funeral, with all its arrangements, is over. It seems to you that you have only kept your heart from breaking because you wanted to see his dear face as long as possible, and there was a feverish anxiety to do all for him that you could. But that is all over now, and the horror of living without him is borne down upon you like a weight that crushes the life out of your heart, and you cry out to the Lord to take you too. But all at once you think of the children, whom, perhaps, he left in your care, and you have just thought of it, and your long habit of endurance for his dear sake comes like a staff upon which you lean, and for his sake and the children's you begin to look about you and wonder how you can win their bread, for after this you must be mother and father in one. No rules can be formulated for such sorrows and perplexities, for each case is peculiar in itself.

It is better for the church that your husband has served, and that should soon have another pastor, that you remove to some other city or village. The removal will be better for yourself and children. It may be a wrench, second only to the death of your husband; but if you do not remove, you will be obliged to take another place in the church, and it will be easier to do it in some other church. If the people follow you with their gifts as well as their prayers until you can find your new place in the world that now seems so dreary to you, do not refuse them. You will be blessed in receiving and they in giving.

What can the widowed pastor's wife do?

The answer depends entirely upon natural qualifications. If health and home duties will permit, perhaps one can go back to teaching. If there is a love for the work, no one could be better fitted for a church or Sunday-school missionary, and the salary ought to be ample so that the worker could become absorbed in her work. We can imagine a sweet and tender intimacy between such a missionary and the pastor's wife of the church served. I recall a missionary who always came to the church meetings early to meet me and confer about her work. I felt while she was our missionary that I had wings and could fly as well as walk to my work; but even in such pure intimacy I learned by a real experience that there were those who thought themselves defrauded of my society, and that I could not be too careful of even the appearance of being more intimate with one church-member than I was with others.

The pastor's wife who learned her lessons well while her husband was living cannot fail to be a very useful person in the church. No one can do more to increase the love of denominational literature, and the editors and book-men can have the advantage of her experience and tact. It is everything in having congenial work, and as success comes, as it surely will, the sorrows of the parting will be absorbed in the joy of meeting in heaven the loved co-worker, who is even now rejoicing over the sheaves his wife is garnering.

The children, not alone her own, but all the children who know her, "will rise up and call her blessed," and after a long and useful life is passed and the pearly gates are opened wide for her abundant entrance, the fragrance of life will be so sweet that the pastor's wife will hardly realize when heaven is reached. And how precious her reward when, hand in hand, she and her loved one hear the Master's welcome: "Well done, good and faithful servant; thou hast been faithful over a few things, I will make thee ruler over many things: enter thou into the joy of thy lord."

.